USA's WASPs:

who are we– really?

by

Joseph Christ

RoseDog Books

PITTSBURGH, PENNSYLVANIA 15238

RoseDog Books
585 Alpha Drive
Pittsburgh, PA 15238
Visit our website at www.rosedogbookstore.com

ISBN: 978-1-4809-7746-4
eISBN: 978-1-4809-7769-3

Dedication: to all you humans, equally

CONTENTS

Books to which I refer are *The Spanish-American War*, *Mexican-American War*, *The War of 1812*, *An American Tragedy* by Dreiser, *Elmer Gantry* by Sinclair Lewis, *The Spanish Civil War* by A. Beevor, *The Prince* by Machiavelli, *Catch-22* by Joseph Heller, *Dune* by Frank Herbert, *Stranger in a Strange Land* by Robert Heinlein, Harper Lee's *Go Set a Watchman*, Arthur Koestler's *Darkness at Noon*, R. M. Pirsig's *Zen and the Art of Motorcycle Maintenance*, R.M. Pirsig's *Lila*, and Tom Wolf's *The Electric Kool-Aid Acid Test*. I believe the scientist's book is *A Beginner's Guide to Reality*. My freshman lit text was *The Modern Age*.

CHAPTER ONE:

The Past of Our Culture

The Greeks about 2,750 or more years ago had the basics of culture which we are using today. That is government to provide needed services and protection, and a market economy to purchase goods, not all necessary. The story *Beowulf* is a good example of the ideal of our culture between the A.D. years 500 to 700. *Beowulf* was written in England in about 700, but it was about Danish and northern European kings and warriors of the 500s. The values expressed are for courage, honesty, modesty, goodness, warrior skills, and getting rich. Behavior is rigidly feudal and very violent. Weapons, swords, and helmets are handed down to sons. Nobles are told to push pride and grow famous and rich. Julius Caesar in conquering Gaul a few years before Christ killed 1,000,000 French humans.

Charlemagne was crowned Emperor of the Roman Empire by the Pope on Christmas Day 800 A.D. The capital of Charlemagne's Empire was Aachen. The Holy Roman Empire ended (in power, not in name) in October 1648 with the Westphalia

Peace which ended the Thirty Years War. This war defeated the Austrian Empire and the central European Catholics.

In 1914 two Caesars, Wilhelm II of Germany and Franz Joseph of Austria-Hungarian Empire, wanted to humiliate the small state of Serbia. So, Austria-Hungary declared war on July 28, 1914, on Serbia. Serbia is peopled by Slavs, so the Russian brothers mobilized for war on July 31. Wilhelm II told his cousin (Actual) Nicholas II to stop mobilizing, but the Czar refused. So, on August 1, Germany declared war on Russia. Then Germany declared war on Russia's treaty ally France on August 2. The next days the German Army marched through Belgium which brought war with King Albert's Belgium and by treaty with Belgium, Great Britain declared war on August 4. World War I lasted until November 11, 1918, when the German government signed an Armistice. With the armistice, the Entendre armies moved to the west bank of the German Rhine River to insure against war. Thus, Germany had to sign the peace treaty offered in June 1919, but they hated it and the treaty was not good or able to be enforced. British generals noted before 1922 that there were significant Germans working for war strength by 1921. This was no peace, only an armistice. Indeed, this wanting to fight on against the West greatly helped Adolf Hitler become Germany's Fuhrer. He was also helped by the troubles of the Great Depression on the German people's ability to live without money. Hitler started the second act, World War II. This war ended in a split Germany who would stay split until 1991. So, the final end to the War Wilhelm II helped start did not formally end until September 1991.

Damascus at 7500 years is the oldest, continuous city on Earth. Marseilles has been a port for 2500 years.

CHAPTER TWO:

May Lose Our Culture Fast or Slowly to Future Techno-Tyranny

The fast way is with the use of nuclear weapons. Ownership of these weapons has grown since 1945. Russia exploded an atom bomb in 1949. Britain joined the club in 1952, France in February 1960 and China in October 1964. In the last twenty years, Near East and Asian countries have gained nukes, while North Korea is selling the technology to those who want it, irrespective. Since October 1962, we have been only minutes away from nuclear destruction, as we are now today. The weapons, now thermonuclear, are still there, only proliferated. Before 1992, one could expect destruction of central Asia, North America, Europe, and possibly Turkey. Today, the USA is the target. We are the Empire (see below). In December 2015, a U.S. nuclear expert told the news that it is only a matter of time, given the availability, of a nuke being detonated against one of our cities.

Since July 1945, there have been over 1300 (1320 by 1984) A-bombs and/or thermonuclear weapons exploded on Earth. I wonder what this fact has to do with the human cancer rate. Given a future exchange of 2000 nuclear weapons between Russia and the USA, I wonder what that calamity would do to Earth's atmosphere. The radiation fallout would probably kill most humans, or all, but would the bombs degrade the air of Earth so that all land life would die? Or maybe the top forms of life on land will be worms, small lizards, or snakes and alligators/crocs (most likely worms will be King).

In 1918-1919 influenza killed 700,000+ Americans. This could be another fast way of depopulation. A third fast way of ruining our culture is a cyber-attack on the USA; this also could happen in a minute. Apparently, our culture is now hopelessly dependent on computers to function, especially finance but also energy and to some extent travel (air).

A big strain to our culture could come in 2092 (approximation) when oil/gasoline will no longer be sold to the public—it will be gone. That is, unless the propaganda is correct (400,000 years of oil for the USA to use), or unless our government prepares for the event. Also, overpopulation will strain the Earth's food and water supplies, but we're rich so we won't starve.

In the 1930s, in the Spanish Civil War, newspapers did not cogently explain the conflict. They sold papers based on sensational stories.

Since 1984, word meaning has changed in the media. Climate change is used for global warming. (Call it what you like, you'll have Hell-fire heat and water up to your ass.) Human nature = evil. Reagan named the new nuclear missile the Peacekeeper. Ethnic cleansing (Slobodan Milosevic) = genocide. Surgical strike = ending disease. Detainee abuse = torture. Beating to death = compassion. Corporation = a person, while humans = a tool. Care in the community = letting the crazies out from hospitals into the community.

In December 1985, George Kennan wrote that the U.S. government debt was crippling to the people's economy and that with the media we may lose our ability to distinguish between the real and unreal. Prior to that, in 1958, one American wrote that there were two problems facing us. One was that we can't deal with advertising. Two, is that technology may sweep off whole orders of life. This technology effect may change the Earth into an unlivable place.

War on terror (is an act, not words) it induces fear which allows control. While in Europe in the summer of 2003, 35,000 people die from heat. Beginning on July 14, 1995, over 740 people, many old, died in the Chicago Heat Wave. The U.S. government research wrongly blamed the victims for their death rather than the extreme weather. Since the 1960s, government agencies and leaders were using plausible denial. Then to 1992 it was used by the CIA, Richard Nixon, Ronald Reagan, and George Bush. Today (2016) it is used very often by the White House. This is unreality—selling a presentable (unreal) image.

In 2002 the U.S. government said there were too many (rich) people to prosecute for fraud, cooked books, and insider trading. In 2003, the government/FBI was looking at all Americans every e-mail, website visited, grade, bank deposit, trip, event purchase with credit card, and magazine subscriptions. They also noted your library books and books bought. At this time politicians in control of government began pushing religious positions, such as intelligent design (by God), to be offered to our children as science. In 2001 President Bush took away medical stem cell research. One writer said in 2005 that we should be in crisis over our government. (In 2004 President George Bush began trying to control government scientists—the truth). In 2004 the Republican administration said on record (at least in front of a reporter) that "We are an Empire now our acts create our own reality." Not only our government is failing us but the news media is too, particularly TV news shows, reporters, and journalists.

Long ago we loved a man who spoke the truth of our government, Will Rogers. In 1921–23, he talked about potential evils in our culture—real estate agents, advertising men, and bankers. He described banking as nonessential. Today, I, or most of you, cannot get money to live without a bank. In 1923, advertising men were the richest in the USA. Will suggested President Warren G. Harding was the most corrupt administration ever. Harding's Interior Secretary was imprisoned for the Teapot Dome Wyoming oil scandal. By 1923, the income of the richest was hidden. Back in 1916, 1296 men earned above $300,000 and paid $1,000,000,000 in taxes. In 1924, Will said what was wanted was just taxes for all. In 1925, congressmen's salaries go from $7500 to $10,000 dollars. November 1927, a seat on the stock exchange cost $300,000.

Noam Chomsky was a very intelligent scientist. When young, I studied some of his theories. In 1970–71 he described the U.S. as a fascist democracy with super powers in the Executive. This makes an elective dictatorship. He said there was an international corporate hegemony in investment. Since 2001, I say this hegemony includes most of the third world countries.

George Kennan in 1989 expressed fear for the deterioration of Earth (by us humans) as supporting life.

A scientist a decade ago spent a book talking about what is known to be real in our world. For example, that the teleporting of photons is science fact. This scientist described our society as having some hyper-real communications, usually the media, electronic or printed page. I call this pseudo-real not hyper-real. Almost always the subject is something we are wanted to believe, whether it is real or not—Like needing that new luxury car.

What I am TRYING TO SAY in the last page is that unless we act to stop the Corporate-Military-political strength of Power (in D.C.) and the lies and recognize Pseudo-reality, we MAY wind up in a future real scene of a place like fictions of: *Logan's Run*, *The Terminator*; *I Have No Mouth, and I Must Scream*, *Soylent Green*, or *THX-1138*.

People, keep your FREEDOMS. "Each new product of capitalism . . . increases swindling and plundering"—Karl Marx, 1844. I hope that not all of you now live and love primarily to buy new things (Mercedes). If so then the advertising men earned their pay. D.D. Eisenhower 1-17-1961: "We must guard against the growth of influence . . . by the military-industrial complex. The potential for the disastrous rise of misplaced power exists and will persist. We must never let . . . this combination endangers our liberties or democratic processes." Chief Justice Earl Warren, 1961: " . . . Temptation to totalitarian security methods must be resisted." They must be as they lower the rights of an individual.

CHAPTER THREE:

England of the 1500s

The Tudors ruled in this century. Henry VIII began ruling in 1509. He and his daughters had a number of powerful people burnt alive at the stake, or beheaded. Notably Henry had the Duke Norfolk burnt in 1547 and Thomas More in 1535. In May 1536, he had Queen Anne (Boleyn) beheaded. Three queens later he married eighteen-year-old Catherine, related to Boleyn. However, he later had Catherine beheaded along with her friends and confidants. King Henry VIII killed or had killed in front of him 72,000 humans. He reigned for over thirty years. In the Spring of 1549, Thomas Seymour was executed. Mary I became Queen in July 1553. Mary had hung the twelve-day Queen Jane. From 1558 to 1603, Queen Elizabeth ruled the government and Parliament. Elizabeth had her cousin, Mary Stuart Queen of Scotland, hanged on February 18, 1587. Ireland fought a battle against English rule on August 15, 1598. Elizabeth was furious and won the battle and the political fight afterwards. The Irish were massacred by famine and war also by Henry Plantagenet as well as Elizabeth Tudor.

Now let's look at the Stuarts who ruled in the 1600s. King Charles I declares war on his own people in August 1642. In October 1642, the first battle is fought against the Puritans. Charles I was beheaded in January of 1649. Britain was a republic from 1648 to 1660. In May 1660, the fleet goes to get King Charles II. In 1666, the Great Plague starts in London (100,000 die). Also in 1666, unlucky number, the Great Fire burns much of London on September 2 to 5. On the 6th, 90 percent of the city was in ashes. In Feb. 1685 Charles II dies, James II becomes King. In November 1688 William of Orange lands in England with a force of 200 ships. The Glorious Revolution begins. On December 23, James II flees to France. His people (Protestant) did not want him.

In England in 1960s to 1970, there was a try at social revolution. A writer in 2001 told us that Britain is now ruled by an elective dictatorship. In 2005 British people's morality is despised, savings is devalued, and patriotism is derided. To many, folk religion is dead. On 7-7-2005, there are bombs across London.

CHAPTER FOUR:

The USA's Government

James Madison was President from 1808 to 1816. In June 1812, the president spoke to Congress for war with Britain. He talked of British violations and illegal acts which were hurting Americans. These were ideals. War was going to cause human suffering and death. Also spoken of was the problem of the northwest Injuns. Taking of Canada was not spoken of but was thought by many. J. Madison must not have been thinking clearly. Great Britain was one of the three most powerful military nations. Her navy had over 1000 warships, the U.S. Navy had 10 large warships. How was this going to turn out? The war against Canada did not go well. Early the British took Detroit away from us. Then in December 1813 they burnt Buffalo to the ground. Finally, in 1814, they invaded and took about half of Maine. Also, they had landed and burnt Washington, D.C. Madison was criminal in not preparing a sound defense of his capital. The war ruined the U.S. economy. By 1814, the government was defaulting on its loans.

Andrew Jackson became president from 1829 to 1837. He was said to have helped the people and the Federal government as a fresh, invigorating personality. However, there were some important men who were afraid in Jackson's presence. This because they (and I) thought he was a killer. In February 1815, after the battle of New Orleans which General Jackson won, he had six men tried and executed who went home before the battle. This is extreme.

Theodore Roosevelt of the Rough Riders rode the Spanish American War to an empire and the presidency. So, it was ill luck taking Guam and Manila in the USA's new empire, which the Japanese would need to secure in an aggression to the south. Thus the U.S. involvement in WW II.

F.D. Roosevelt in his Fated Interlude reign (See the book *Fated Interlude*) made one important significant error. A U.S. leader knew it was wrong to not stop giving Lend Lease aid to the USSR in June 1944, when the Red Army began advancing west out of Russia. Many German leaders, like General von Mellenthin, thought the same. Diplomat George Kennan said that on July 1, 1944, the USA failed by not stopping Lend-Lease to the USSR. Early in the Korean War, there was disagreement between President Truman and General McArthur. Truman won the argument, and we have had more than sixty-five years of North Korean aggressive crazy and since the '90s nuclear proliferation. John Kennedy had to prove he was tough against communism so in the early '60s he increased the U.S. military presence in South Vietnam—a mistake.

President Richard Nixon appears to have committed crimes, against the people at least, in the '60s and '70s. President from 1981–89, Ronald Reagan was suffering from significant brain damage (Alzheimer's). Ronald Reagan died in June 2004 with Alzheimer's. President Reagan did not understand for years that Mikhail Gorbachev was sincere in changes of Russia's policies and that he (Gorbachev) wanted to increase cooperation with the USA. The 2000 to 2008 President, George Bush II, made mistakes that I believe damaged us. In 2004, President George W. Bush's administration compared oil companies' growth to increasing freedom, and that poor countries were obligated to give the U.S. new investment so that we take over their water, electricity, food, and industries. President Bush started wars that have lasted for fifteen years. Do you think that is good? I don't. I seem to remember having more freedoms in 2000 than today. In 2017, we got a new president. He reminds me. In the September 1930 election, Adolf Hitler won many votes with a program like "We will make America strong again." Only he lived in another country.

CHAPTER FIVE:

The USA's Expansion and Grabbing

Before the 1812 War, many influential men were expansionists. These men wanted the Injuns pushed out of the northwest (then around Michigan) and possibly to take Canada from Britain. In the West, the hunting of buffaloes reduced them to an endangered species by 1880.

In 1844 an expansionist James K. Polk was elected president. March 1, 1845, the U.S. annexes the Texas Republic. The Texas legislature eventually agrees. Mexico protests this and cuts off diplomatic relations with the U.S. Polk sends General Z. Taylor with troops to Texas. Taylor then marches into Mexico on the Rio Grande. In April 1846, Zachary Taylor's men fight Mexican soldiers, eleven Americans are killed. Polk uses this as a declaration of war that he gives to Congress. The President speaks wrongly, claiming Mexico started the war spilling "American blood upon American soil." The war with Mexico begins.

In June 1846, U.S. settlers in California led by Colonel Fremont revolt against Mexico and set up the Bear Flag Republic.

Mexicans in California fight the U.S., and California is not secured until January 1847 when U.S. troops take and control Los Angeles. The U.S. Army invades and takes Mexico's capital Mexico City. The capital is secured on September 14, 1847. With the peace treaty of February 1848, the U.S. gets the Rio Grande border, New Mexico, and California, for which they pay Mexico $15,000,000.

In 1848, the USA offered Spain $100,000,000 for the rich island of Cuba. Spain turned it down. In 1868, Cuban natives rebelled against its Spanish rulers. The revolt lasted for ten years. Revolutionary Cuban exiles came to New York, where they stirred up feelings and support for Cuban independence. The U.S. people had perhaps $50,000,000 invested in Cuban businesses. In February 1895, a new insurrection began. The press, like Joe Pulitzer and W. Randolph Hearst, loved the Cuban revolution news. This helped make substantial public support for the native Cubans. This substance influenced Congress. More expansionists came to power in March 1897, Republicans under William McKinley. McKinley helps Spain decide to offer Cuba political autonomy, some freedom. The Cuban rebels reject this idea. In March 1898, the U.S. offered to buy Cuba from Spain, again. Spain rejected this. Congress was increasingly interventionist about Cuba. April 19, 1898, Congress passed a joint resolution for recognition of Cuban independence. This meant war. On April 23, Spain declared war. On April 25, the U.S. followed suit.

Puerto Rico was a unique colony in 1898. She had more control over her governing, as did Australia. She enjoyed rights not had by Spanish in Spain. Her autonomy included a legislative assembly. In 1898, the U.S. government wanted Puerto Rico. The

U.S. Army began landing on July 25. Within days, a rebel commission gained about 2500 volunteers to serve the USA as Puerto Rican Scouts. The people of Ponce port made a hospital for the American wounded. In a town inland, friendly natives made an infirmary to care for suffering U.S. troops. The USA won the war. The peace treaty of December 10, 1898, gave the USA Puerto Rico, Guam, and the Philippines, for which the U.S. gave Spain $20,000,000.

On July 6, 1898, the U.S. Congress completed the votes on annexation of Hawaii. McKinley signed this into law and had an Army regiment, the 1st New York, put ashore to occupy the Islands. This was not really needed. But many Hawaiians today resent us Howlies. Shortly, the USA annexed Wake Island, Midway Island, and other mid-Pacific islands.

Spanish nobles had ruled the Philippine Island for 300+ years. But in May 1898, when Admiral Dewey with fleet sat in Manila Bay there were 30,000 armed native insurgents under their commander Emilio Aguinaldo. In 1896, native Tagalogs began the revolt. This revolution was for independence. They fought hard through 1897 but were defeated. In 1897, Aguinaldo made a manifesto, Biyakna-Bato, demanding reforms, autonomy—not independence—in the Empire, and racial equality. By December 1897, the natives and Spain had agreed to these. But in March 1898, the U.S. Navy talked with Aguinaldo about support in the Philippines for a war against Spain. In further talks with a U.S. diplomat, Aguinaldo agreed to help. He thought they had agreed to native independence under U.S. protection. May 24, Aguinaldo was back in the Philippines leading the insurgents and declaring himself dictator of the people's revolution. By the end of May, he had a strong 30,000 insurgents. The insurgents, helped by the U.S. Army, eventually blockaded the Spanish forces in Manila. The native rebels on June 12, 1898, led by Aguinaldo, proclaimed a new independent Republic of the Philippines. Aguinaldo then sought to establish government organizations. These acts of independence the U.S. military ignored. In December 1898, Spain gave without a hindrance or lien the Philippines to the USA. The U.S. Congress in 1934 gave independence to the Philippines. Independence was to start on July 4, 1946. The Philippines people were not allowed in on these peace talks in 1898. Were the natives so primitive? This is the argument the English made after Darwin's science of evolution in the nineteenth century. The natives of Africa particularly, but also of Asia and the Pacific islands were under-evolved relative to the fine British culture. Therefore, it was the Christian duty of the English to guide and control (exploit) them. Apparently, the Americans bought this. Is this true today? Your vote here:

CHAPTER SIX:

The USA with Others and Race Relations

In 1813, General Andrew Jackson led troops in war against the Creek Indians on the southern frontier. The Creek Indians were a more civilized organization of natives than other Indians—they practiced agriculture, raised livestock, and had an effective form of government. After slaughtering the Creek in war, Jackson forced them to sign a treaty which stripped them of over half of their territory.

A large number of Americans who fought in Mexico and New Mexico felt superior to the Mexicans they were fighting. Most thought Mexicans were lazy, ignorant, and not fit to rule over white people. This fits with the newspapers trumpeting Manifest Destiny—the God-given right of the white U.S. to take and "civilize" all of North America.

President James Monroe, 1816 to 1824, made no hindrance to wealthy black Americans, mostly freed slaves, who made a West African country, Liberia, in 1822. Monroe as former Secretary of State knew foreign relations. Liberia was created more with help of U.S. colonization societies. Monroe Doctrine of 1823 protects American revolutions from European Royalties and powers.

In June 1846 when the American people led by Colonel Fremont started the California Republic there were only 700 Americans while there were 8,000 Mexicans and about 90,000 Injuns living in the California region.

In the fall of 1898, the American people were informed of the peace negotiations going on with Spain. Some, liberals and intellectuals did not want an Empire. At the other end of the spectrum were Americans who did not want the annexations to pollute America with non-whites. Still the peace treaty passed the Senate comfortably. Writing of Hawaiians disliking whites, I was told by a kindly native realtor, a female, not to move into a local neighborhood because I would be hated.

Abraham Lincoln in 1863 set the blacks free. This is two years after Czar Alexander set the Russian serfs free. From 1865 to 1877, after the war the Union helped the Southern blacks prosper and live freely. Black men served in state legislatures. One black man served in the federal Congress. In 1876, there was a close presidential race. There were strong feelings on both sides for the candidates. Republican Rutherford B. Hayes won the presidency. He began, probably corruptly, to serve in March 1877. To win by five electoral-college votes, Hayes gave to two Southern states power to the old rulers. So, on 4-10-1877, the Union leaves. Taking the Union troops out of the South leaves the white supremacists and the KKK in charge. Shortly this led to black neck-tie parties—the lynching of "uppity" blacks. These lynchings and court rulings sentencing regularly against blacks went on through the 1940s. These social conflicts went on with mass white agreement, but there were some white Southern folk opposed. Harper Lee was an Alabama girl who wrote a novel published in 1960. This won her many awards. She had written a novel in about 1953 which she thought inferior and refused to publish. This story, *Set a Watchman*, gives me insight into the prejudices of the common white Southerner. It was believed that 1. Blacks were socially less capable, 2. They could not learn well enough to counter this problem and, 3. That to include them in our society, particularly schools, would greatly damage it.

For 12,000 years prior to 1859, when cities started in Washington Territory, humans lived on the Columbia River to live off its salmon population. The Northwest natives, the Bering Ice Bridge Asians, have lived in North America for 15,000 years. These were Ice Age peoples running south from the ice. They eventually sparsely settled North and South Americas. In the warmth, these people formed at least three civilizations, the Aztec, Mayan and Inca. In the Northwest, these humans had—when American settlers came in from the Oregon Trail—homes, dogs, pottery, cloth and bows and arrows. These humans were living not 80,000 years after the first Homo sapiens. Note that if or when the Fifth Ice Age starts do not plan on a beach party birthday.

I am impressed in the Northwest that there are so many public schools named after great Injun chiefs. Also, that you rarely see an Injun loose around here. In, I think the 1960s, a California college professor, also ethnically an Injun, said to us "They put the Injun away . . . yeah it's part of the Jesus scheme." One English writer post WW II described the U.S. treatment of Injuns as genocide and wondered why no one had said so.

An unintended consequence of white peoples living with the natives was greatly reduced native populations due to diseases they had no immunity to. A large percentage of American Natives died from diseases that were introduced unwittingly. In 1778, when Captain Cook came to Hawaii, there were 400,000 Oahuans. In 1865, there were only 55,000 Oahuans.

In 1906 the Japanese were incensed by the San Francisco Schools segregating their Japanese student children. This created bad feelings between the two nations for some years. December 8, 1941, on Wake Island, a Pan Am Clipper was taking off with all passengers and employees. Employees not allowed on the Clipper were Guam natives, the Chamorros (the non-whites). The IJN had just bombed the Island.

In 1947, black man Jackie Robinson BROKE through into N.L. baseball with the Brooklyn Dodgers, champions in '47. This was done in spite of opposition of racist white ballplayers (and many fans); one of the racist leaders was teammate Dixie Walker, RF. Jackie was the first black professional (paid) ballplayer in the white leagues.

CHAPTER SEVEN:

Who Are We

One author described 1840–1860 American thought as centering on education and including evangelisms and sects. In 1860, there was no unemployment, overproduction, or lack of market. In 1900, there were no "No Trespassing" signs. In 1901, the Democratic Party now believed that business should be helped, but discreetly. From 1900 on, cattle ranches and produce farms were lowering in strength and success, while rising in strength were manufactures, mortgages, and businessmen.

In the 1930s, our cousins the British used companies to gain profits from beating the blockade (of Spain's Civil War) made by the European governments. The British Conservative Party was not really committed to democracy abroad, particularly in Spain. The British "well to do" were for General Franco and the Nationalists throughout the War. A Welshman, Dylan Thomas, in the '30s wrote of the British capitalist society that it has made men a bundle of repressions and useless habits. Also, he writes of the snob of country gentry and the family tree dedicated by old totems and fetishes of possessions. Mr. Thomas has one character say, "Marriage, legal monogamous prostitution." A Britisher writing after WW II of America humorously described our government as not located in Washington, D.C., but around Wall Street. Americans are taught in institutions how to be delinquent without breaking the law. These institutions are called law schools. The upper levels of U.S. government are dominated by lawyers. In 1993, 3,000,000 poor die a year while with cloning we maintain yuppie/rich zygotes and make backup copies and freeze for organs or maybe take them from the poor.

In 1914, one writer described our urban workers as skeptical and apathetic. I, in 2015, describe those Americans I see as selfish, showing signs of aggression and hatred (especially behind the wheel) behind a false cover of goody-goodiness. There are many who believe they are truly acting for good, such as giving to charities and occasionally to the needy. But giving meals to the poor does not really help much. The poor need help when they are younger, like in kindergarten on up. They need brothers and sisters, love like Jesus.

A British writer, Les James, in 1950 wrote a book in which he described Americans. Humorously, he said we had a compulsive need to consume. That we had more than our just share of the world's goods, and that U.S. Congress was run by "pressure groups." Richard Nixon gave some support for this when he said in 1970 that the USA consumed most of the world's energy (about 70 percent).

Apparently, Christianity offers riches in the next world, not so much in this. The Christian dogma of rewards in the afterlife may have been used after 1789 in the West to keep the growing poor under control during their lives. This was done by the wealthy in power. I believe Karl Marx attacked this by denying an afterlife. The Russian USSR leaders in the 1950s mocked us with "There will be pie in the sky when you die."

Christianity had always been a powerful factor in all the N. American English colonies. In the 1600s and 1700s, religious leaders controlled the behavior of people of powerful individualism and those who thought and behaved away from their standards. They sought conformity and to punish any deviance. They burnt "witches." Then the USA was nearly alike in the cultural norms with Great Britain, Canada, and Australia from 1790 on. The English were very refined, subdued, correct (repressed) during the reign of Victoria. This gave us the culture of Victorianism. This culture lasted until WW I in 1918. The Great War was a powerful cultural shock. The fundaments of Victorianism were mostly replaced by something like science/technology/University professions. This led to changes in organizations, views, goals, leaders and behaviors. F. D. Roosevelt played an important part in some changes of organizations and goals. FDR was hated by some conservatives (the Right). Social behaviors were most affected. Repression was lifted to the concern of parents and older generations. Playing, dancing, flirting and SEX were now done more openly. Driving cars, boats and flaunting your wealth was now the vogue (1920s). The conflict between generations was prominent so much that it became a plot in many books (Zane Grey) and movies in the 1930s. The conflict between generations lasted after WW II and is with us today. Talk to teachers about the control and respect they get from their students. Some get it, but many are short of it. This was more pronounced in the '70s to '90s.

Zane Grey was ambivalent in his descriptions of our Injuns. Zane wrote very popular/influential novels beginning in 1907. Sometimes he described hateful Injun behaviors of great brutality and barbarity. But he also spent time writing of the positive behavior code that included courage, bravery facing destruction and silent truthfulness and determination. R.M. Pirsig wrote that he believes Americans have taken this behavior code as to their own.

CHAPTER EIGHT:

Our Anti-cultures

In 1915, with the horror of WW I on, in Switzerland there began a new art form. Switzerland was a haven surrounded by warring countries. One name of this was Dadaist art. Art bizarre, beyond the rules which given the horror of War, was now true to the human psyche. After WW I many Allied men who saw the war became part of what was called the Lost Generation. These men were alienated and anomic. They and writers and artists stayed in Paris and made an impact on our culture (Hemmingway, the writer of *Tropic of Capricorn*, and Dos Passos) and F.S. Fitzgerald in America. A freshman text of mine states that the postwar decade with the Lost Americans was filled by government corruption, disillusionment, the new jazz, lawlessness and great philistinism. Bob-haired girls talked about sex, dressed like boys, and cursed and behaved like them. Throughout America, the young were restless and rootless—having given up Victorianism. It is interesting that with a far more limited population these behaviors of young women took place 60 years before in the 1860s in Petersburg Russia with political Social Revolutionaries. These women were far freer than the normal Russian regarding, sex and marriage and smoked cigarettes and wore their hair bobbed.

In 1918, some Americans sympathized with the socialist Republic (in Russia). In the 1920s, some British did too. This sympathy lasted until 1950 when it became clear that Stalinism crazily repressed everyone under Stalin's totalitarian regime. There were no freedoms, no socialism in Russia, only the Party ruled by the iron fist of Stalin. But individuals believed as "fellow travelers" in Russia's socialism up through the 1940s. Think of the powerful beliefs for Socialism and against their own governments to allow American and British scientists to give the A-bomb to Stalin and Russia.

From the 1930s on, our American families changed in that divorce caused breakups, re-forming, and new families. Wives now knew that they could (with some censure) get out of bad relationships. So, this new freedom caused some problems with adjustment. Humans need long term relationships. With our new culture and powers to move (automobiles, jobs) we lost some of our security and stability. Our kids were particularly affected. By 1951, our children, some of, were rebelling against authority, more at school than at home. Some were delinquent, law breakers. By 1960, some refused to obey school officials. Often the refuser was not a good student but was talented some other way, usually physically. So, these rebels were admired by their peers for their selves and for standing up to the teacher. Quite so, the feelings against control grew. In the 1980s, there were children who would not work for the teacher. They simply refused to with some teachers. I saw a destructive rebellion in

1990 when the students of a class ruined all the teacher's computers. By the '90s some students had no qualms about cheating rather than learning. I was told the grade was the same.

By 1960 on, more kids, usually older, were rebelling against family and college authority. It grew markedly from 1964 to 1974. Those in control were concerned by 1965 with these confrontations to their authority. The rebelling or young movement spread to London, Paris, Prague, and Italy. Prague, Czechoslovakia, was in the East, a Commie place where a rebellion broke out in 1968. Even in Communist Yugoslavia, on June 3–4, 1968, the young and university's made demonstrations and sit-ins. U.S. college campuses were sites of protests, sit-ins, marches and some revolts. Three Ohio students were shot and killed in 1970. Our students were protesting against the Vietnam War, against capitalism, the System, and against controls on their lives.

From the 1920s on in the cities there were some WASPs who tried drugs, some used occasionally. After WW II particularly in the 1950s drug experiments and usage gained in youth and WASPs. These gains were helped by the spirit of youth resistance. In the 1950s, the first rather large anti-cultures appeared. These were called beatniks and the Hell's Angels bikers. The media picked up on the beatniks and gave us the ideas of them from movies and TV shows, like from 1959 to 1962 with Maynard G. Krebs and Dobie. With the beatniks were supposedly dropouts, witches, sexually different and other rebels, like musicians. The Hell's Angels were largely ex-servicemen traumatized by war. The beatniks were youth who did not like the cultures "scene." These were interested in "cool" rather than making money, or fitting in to the slot society wanted. There became a bohemian world in some cities. As an example of this difference, Jack Kerouac wrote of hitchhiking. Kerouac's hero was Neal Cassidy. Cassidy was racing through life and back and forth across North America. By 1964, he was a "speed freak."

Then after 1963 came the hippies and broad and deep drug usage. This was a major anti-culture. The hippies were against Power, authority, and Position. In 1965-66 there was a psychedelic movement. This was opening the mind with LSD-25, peyote buttons, DMT, and/or mescaline. Some compared this to St. Paul and the early Christians. Aldous Huxley had compared the brain to a reducing valve. The brain filters down the senses perceptions to a level we can deal with, apprehend (See the Last chapter). Thus, we are shut off from the World. Huxley said the drugs opened these doors/filters and gave us the Divine—That which Words Cannot Describe. This may open you to the Universe. It also makes you appear mad, crazy to others who aren't using.

Ken Kesey led this psychedelic movement. In July 1964, he and his (12) Travelers crossed the USA in his Day-Glo bus, doing drugs all the way. High out in the open of America these screaming, insane Pranksters were freaking out the sedate citizens. Their destination was Furthur. These Travelers were so synched that they had some telepathic powers. Kesey, like Valentine Michael Smith, shares everything with his people, like a pot of money at the door. These people experienced ESP phenomenon. They were synchronized together. They used the I Ching, the book of Changes. Kesey is talking about the 1/30 second lag between your senses and mind.

In October 1965, Ken Kesey talked to college students at the U Cal Vietnam Day. He advised to turn your backs to it and say,

"Fuck it." Later, in 1965, Kesey and the Pranksters started the Acid tests. This was turning on large groups of people to the Acid experience. There were about fifteen Acid tests. A great one was in San Francisco December 5, 1965. Kesey's movement was over by 10-31-1966. At least his person and control was gone. So, it was no longer pure and sort of religious as a brotherhood. But, in San Francisco, January 21–23, 1966, the Trips Festival opened up the LSD experience to the whole public. Now there were many Acid Heads around California. February 1966, business entrepreneur Bill Graham made Acid and Acid Rock a money making personal Experience for large groups of youth. He was holding a Trips Festival every weekend. Janis Joplin was one of their (SF Acid) top musicians (a Singer). Soon this was on the cover of *Life* magazine with Acid Heads/Trips. Then TV and newspapers began informing the public of these events/experiences. The acid/LSD scene reached England in December 1966 —the Beatles. The Beatles in 1967 led a social change movement with their media Magical Mystery Tour. Actually, they bought a bus and drove it around the country and let people on the bus, taking drugs like Kesey and Travelers. These events were a social and mental revolution going against our culture. The original leader of this revolution was Ken Kesey who tried hard to change, improve the human social world. Ultimately he failed.

So, after 1970, there have always been a small proportion of our people who took drugs and did not believe all of our culture or behave completely legally. There were communes in college towns in the 1970s. There were young people living together sharing food, drugs, and money. The percentage of people in this anti-culture has varied, I am guessing, from 5 to 33 percent, depending on where you are and what year. Not all on drugs but not believing or behaving with the norm/expected. These were usually young but some grew up and had families. Perhaps in the '80s, 10–15 percent were using while it has gone down generally since.

This anti-culture contains 6 major factors. These are freedoms in sex and drugs and behaviors in public schools and colleges. Three factors are the media of—music, TV and the movies. These media suggest to Americans, particularly the young, liberal freedoms and resistance to authority and religious restrictions. Thus, the Religious Right has been, since 1980 at the latest, trying to gain political control of the people in Congress and with the Presidency. Religion is fighting American human's behavioral freedoms. So, since 1970 we have had a bifurcated population with opposing differences. Thus, Presidents can be in complete (?) opposition to America's young—George Bush I's war on drugs, "just say NO." Our youths' attitudes reflect this bifurcation with skeptical-ness, personal freedoms, but within our culture while making money (that what's this life's about).

Tom Wolf in *The Electric Kool-Aid Acid Test* tells us from the early '60s into the '70s we have had the Probation generation. This is after the Beat Generation and the Lost Generations. The youth opposition and the media factors grew in synch from the '70s on. Pink Floyd gave us music of teacher's making, with punishments, mind control over the students. Occasionally in movies there are references or hints of the broad social conflicts. In Mike Douglas' 1984 movie, he asks a girl if she's smoked pot. Joan Wilder says, "Yes, I went to college." A family member two generations after me appears to have minored in pot in her freshman year.

I remember the 1970s as a time when a large percentage of men I knew under thirty-five took drugs and did not always obey the laws. In college, there were always skeptics of our culture and drug users. When I lived in a dorm, the other youths, by the dozens, pressured me to smoke pot. Finally, to shut them up, I did a few times. But then so did Bill Clinton.

CHAPTER NINE:

Our Struggles with Other Forms of Governmen

In Britain in the nineteenth century, the Fabians became the Labor Party. In 1883, Gregori Plekhanov started the first Russian Marxist party. In 1890, the German Social Democratic Party was strong with 1.43 million votes. However, these votes made no difference to the Kaiser. In the USA in 1886, the Chicago Riot contained many socialists and anarchists. There were Populists organized politically by 1888. However, the Populist platform was absorbed by the Democrats and Republicans in the 1896 election.

Russia had a so-called Socialist Republic from November 1917 to December 1991. (So-called because the Party acted criminally. These Bolsheviks killed millions of their own people, no more than 9 million in one act. Obviously they did not need votes. Then in the '30s they slaughtered, through fake trials, their own leaders.) A first Russian Revolution started in January 1905 and lasted through December. Czar Nicholas was forced to give the people concessions. When he felt safe, he took them away (the Duma). The last cause of the 1905 revolution was the suffering from the war with Japan. The second revolution was more successful for the people. It started in the Great War. The people had suffered for years. On March 8, 1917, the people acted. The revolt began with women in St. Petersburg. The bourgeois middle class took over the Provisional government and continued to fight the war. The Communists (Bolsheviks) staged a coup in November 1917. Lenin took power. In 1775, the North American revolution took place. It was the English colonists' revolt from the government of King George III. The U.S. revolution was won on 4-3-1783.

The first and completely successful revolution in France started in Paris in July 1789. King Louis knew the people had won over the government of Paris when they on the 14th stormed the Bastille and successfully took away the prisoners. Bourgeois lawyers tried to gain control over the revolution in September 1789 but failed. The middle-class reaction did not gain control over the Directory (government) until the 1790s. Then in November 1799, control of France was given to General Napoleon Bonaparte.

Paris during the war with Germany in 1870–71 was run by a People's Commune. The commune took power in September 1870 with Napoleon III giving up his Empire. Surrounded by a fighting/shelling German Army, the Commune stubbornly held on until January 28, 1871. With the siege, 30,236 Parisians starved to death. French Republicans helped the Germans with the siege of Paris. About 60,000 people were killed during the siege. Starting in February 1848 the proletariat of Paris revolted against authority until June. They were successful in getting Louis Philippe to abdicate. But the bourgeois Provisional Government of the new republic stopped the people's insurgents. Also in 1848, there were revolts in Berlin, Vienna, Prague and Milan.

In 1820, a revolution overthrew the Crown of Spain and formed a revolutionary government. This government was crushed by the army/bourgeois reaction in 1823. This reaction was helped greatly by the French King Louis who sent an army to stamp out the Spanish freemen.

In the New World in 1821, a revolution in Mexico took power from its Spanish masters. In 1817, the people of Brazil made a revolution against their masters from Portugal and won their independence.

The next century, in 1910, the people of Portugal revolted and over threw their monarch and declared a new republic. Beginning in 1910, there was a revolution in Mexico to overthrow the authoritarian government of their dictator Victorio Huerta. The USA helped the Mexican government. In 1911, the Chinese people, under Sun Yat-sen and his Koumintang Nationalist Party, overthrew their empress and took over the government. Beginning in 1896, the people of the Philippines, led by Emilio Aguinaldo, started an insurgent revolt against their Spanish rulers. These insurgents fought alongside the U.S. military who invaded the Philippines in May 1898 to drive out the Spanish. Then in February 1899, the Tagalog insurrectionists began fighting the U.S. military for control of the Philippines. This civil war lasted into 1902.

The Spanish Civil War (1936–39) was fought between the rich powers and the common people. The Republic was disliked by conservatives (Winston Churchill) in England and France. The workers were suppressed/controlled by the Civil Guard, which by 1930 numbered 30,000. To the local workers, these guardsmen were foreigners controlled by the rich.

Europe made a Non-Intervention Committee which proved a farce. The U.S. ambassador to Spain said the Committee is the most cynical and dishonest group ever known. The army coup/revolt was first greatly helped by Adolf Hitler's sending Ju-52s to fly troops from Africa to Spain. Later Hitler sent a few pocket battleships to make Franco's sea transports safe and to shell the Republican ports. Hitler helped the most by training the Spanish Army in 1937. Finally, Hitler sent the Condor Legion of military to greatly increase the Nationalist fighting strength. The Nationalist/fascist cause was also helped by the Royal Navy (who hated revolts of the common sailors) who gave Franco the use of their Gibraltar communications net and had the *BB Queen Elizabeth* placed in front of a Nationalist valuable port to prevent Republican navy shelling. The U.S. and British businesses gave the Nationalists greatly needed credit and oil to fight the war. The U.S. corporations in Spain were ITT, Ford, and GM. Helping the Nationalist cause were Texaco, Standard Oil, and Du Pont. Less profiting was Studebaker, which sent trucks. Apparently, the lesson from this Spanish history is that the USA and Great Britain like more, and are like, Nationalist F. Franco than a government of the common (poor) people.

Chapter Ten:

Last Religion

The idea of Hell was alive in Rome, in at least one play, 200 years before Jesus Christ. The first Christmas was celebrated in Rome in 336 A.D. This may be when the lying started. Jesus was born April 1. In the 1500s in the Tudors' reign, Christians under Luther were demanding reforms in the church. The Roman Emperor, also the Pope, would not listen, and there were protests, strongest in Germany and cities like Nuremburg. Here those who protested took the name of Protestants.

Nicco Machiavelli was published in 1513. He wrote lessons for Italian politicians. His book was hated by liberals and religious believers but appears to have honesty, truth without cant. The Prince says that men are scoundrels and lose their honor so must be kept with fear, the dread of pain. A prince may lie to men since they are usually evil and would not keep a pledge to you, you need not as well. Machiavelli cited Pope Alexander VI as a good example of this. This Pope "never gave thought to anything but deception . . ." A prince may act "in the name of religion" to commit horrible cruelties to foreign peoples. In 1492, Rodrigo Borgia became Pope Alexander. From 1492, Machiavelli believes the Catholic Church definitely turned away from religion to the powers of this world; money/riches, arms, influence and control—this to the detriment of religious believers. This makes Martin Luther's acts more cogent.

History offers some support of Machiavelli's beliefs of the Roman Church. In the twentieth century, Popes supported Nationalist F. Franco's (horrible) acts against the common Spanish people, in the '20s supported the policies of Mussolini in Italy, and finally approved of Hitler's suppression of communism in 1933. The Pope (Pius XI) never found a Fascist dictator he couldn't like. These dictators suppressed freedoms at home and killed many foreigners. Italy gassed many Ethiopians. Francisco Franco's military and police killed 1,000,000 Spanish Republicans over the War and shortly after.

A history of Spain gives us the following. The Catholic Church in Spain, led by Cardinal de Cisneros, helped drive the Moors out by 1492. De Cisneros acted without Rome due to Spain's rejection of the papacy for its corruption. The Church was one of the important foundations of the civilization from 1492 to 1932. In 800, there were 14 million people in Spain. By 1800 there were 7 million people. This is because the peasants' food supply was ruined. Grains had been produced, but the war cost money, which the powers got from selling sheep's wool. Peasants were turned from farmers to shepherds. The people were also controlled by the Church. The Church controlled education. As the army conquered the new world the Church integrated the people into the Empire with the Christian religion.

The Spanish people were under the threat of Hell and the Inquisition. Beevor said that "the promise of heaven for the meek" was played by the rich/powerful to make the poor accept their lot.

By 1904, the Church had one third of the wealth of Spain. Spain's anarchist force was strong. Anarchists believed that the domination of one human by another was the source of all social evil. Anarchism offered a moral alternative to the hypocritical Church. A. Beevor tells us the teachings of the Catholic Church amounted to mental repression. Only a small percentage of laborers attended Church services. Illiteracy was from 25 percent to 50 percent in the regions. The Church was hated by workers for preaching acceptance of poverty while the Church was so rich. The Republic changed the constitution to limit the Church's power. These acts led the Church to be attacked by workers in a revolt. The Church, in an early 1936 election, backed the right, near-fascist coalition of the National Front. The Church said a vote for them was a vote for Christ.

During the civil war, an English volunteer was disconcerted by a priest screaming at the troops to "shoot more of the atheist rabble" (quote of A. Beevor). Pope Pius gave total official support in 1936 for Franco and the Nationalists in the War. After the War, Father Torrent was a supporter of mass executions of Republican Spanish.

This paragraph is conjectural but by 500 B.C. there was a new religion, sort of, in China. There was a great wise man called Lao Tsu who lived his life over 160 years and wrote the Tao Te Ching books. Lao Tsu taught of the Way and of virtue. His teachings were toward human self-effacement. The Way is now described as The Way that can be spoken of is not the way; the way is for ever nameless. The Way begets the One—which creates the universe. "the sage embraces the One" "it is capable of being the mother of the world. I know not its name so I style it THE WAY." "Those who are good I treat as good. Those who are not good I also treat as good. In so doing I gain in goodness." See lessons 41, 42 and 45. Self-effacement is acting without ego. It includes a being opposite to the way human nature expects you. And yet this way of being brings success in the world of people. Antithetical thoughts are true, such as "Deal with a thing while it is still nothing." Lao Tsu says, "One who possesses virtue in abundance is comparable to a new born babe."

This is too deep. But R. M. Pirsig wrote of this in the 1970s. I don't think he got the response he wanted since I have never heard of capital-Q Quality spoken of socially. His Quality was as was the Way. There is a fraction of a second between sensing something and being aware of it. Thus, everything we are aware of is in the past. The cutting edge of reality is the Way-Quality. "Reality is always the moment of vision before" our mind is aware. All of our mind's intellectuality must come from this pre-intellectual reality = the Way. Quality is the "parent" of all the universe. Quality makes the mythos. Men are made by religion=Quality.

Our science author of ten years ago gives science which supports this. He described many strange things unbelievable, impossible occurring in Reality and being lost when our mind becomes aware—things such as virtual particles which are real but we can't usually see. In Reality, we may see ghosts, alternate or impossible events in a strange world. He describes these as: in our world superpositions come into our brain and our mind collapses their wave function so we do not perceive them. Apparently, he tells us, the empty space of our solar system is filled with, though we cannot perceive it, virtual particles. These particles should not be in this world and these our pre-intelligence perceives. An experiment to prove the Uncertainty Principle found the (same) electron passing through both the prepared measurement slits at THE SAME TIME.

Jesus, the Christ, was teaching his lessons 2000+ years ago. People who knew him and He Himself called him the Lamb of God. He taught that the key to the kingdom of God was in all of us. Not outside in some capital like Rome. This spirit of God in us he called the Holy Ghost. Jesus sent his people out to preach the coming of the kingdom of God. Jeshua preached that if you accepted the Holy Spirit within you and became as a little child you were saved. If you valued things over people or were a hypocrite, today's word meaning not truthful to people, or to yourself but pretending to be, you were not saved. I believe Jesus wanted all people to be brothers, ALL not just Jews. One of Jesus' strong acts suggests He did not value capitalism as much as He did spirit and people.

Joan of Arc was born about 1412 in Lorraine. She was killed by the Catholic Church in late May 1431 for heresy and witchcraft. This same church made her Saint Joan in 1920. Joan of Arc did two great things. Politically, she made Charles VII King of France. As a military leader, she led the French army to force England out of central France. Joan's strength was derived she said from voices and visions she got from God. This the Church could not tolerate. She was a rebel[1]. The Inquisition provided

---

[1] (From Authority – she was a strong individual)

men to help the trial of Joan's guilt. Inquisitors were needed as others did not have the Apostolic Succession. Joan stood by her messages from God against the Church, this cost her her life at the stake/fire. They found her against the Lord the Pope. The Holy Father the Pope of Rome was the latest Apostolic Succession.

In the twentieth century, some fine American writers have written about the religion in the USA. Sinclair Lewis' novel of the 1920s had a pastor leaving his church with the words "that no one in this room, including your pastor, believes in the Christian religion. Not one of us would turn the other cheek. Not one of us would sell all that he has and give to the poor. Not one of us would give his coat to some man who took his overcoat. Every one of us lays up all the treasure he can." We do not practice the religion of Christ. I have never seen a man give all or most of his wealth to the poor. My neighborhood is all Christian: we don't let in any poor and we have a binding legal contract to increase the wealth of our homes. This capitalist doctrine is at the cost of personal freedoms. Welcome to the twenty-first century.

Theodore Dreiser wrote *An American Tragedy*. This story of a male born about 1900 in a very religious evangelical family is of the failure of religious belief. Religion does not protect the boy from desires for the physical love of a female or for the good things wealth can give to the very rich. The American boy wanted these things so much that he committed murder to a girl and his child to keep his plan for the riches of life in this world alive. Apparently, Christianity offers riches in the next world, not in this. Though raised with this idea the boy wanted the physical sensations of wealth in this world—WHILE ALIVE. This was the early '20s when he solved the pregnancy problem with murder.

Today we have legal abortions (temporarily?) and in Washington state legal protections (common law marriage) for the wife. Our religion has made some sex and pregnancies a sin. Why not make them all a sin? It would be equal for all like that.

Since WW II, some fiction has tried to address religion. Joseph Heller's *Catch-22* was one. Also, Tacoma writer Frank Herbert wrote, *Dune*, a far futuristic sci-fi novel giving us a new god, Paul Muad'Dib. In *Stranger in a Strange Land* in 1961, Robert Heinlein gave us Valentine Michael Smith, a human-Martian. These gods are not believable, but V.M. Smith did apply Jesus' sharing very well. All were equal as brothers and sisters.

The Ex-communist Arthur Koestler has a communist character say in 1939, can you name one "state which really followed a Christian policy?" The true answer appears to be no. If Christ were being followed today, there would be no great gaps between classes and wealth. Capitalism would be less pervasive. Poor would be able to fly airlines to get that perfect cardboard carton to live in. The following is conjectural; I am guessing as to the changes from Jesus' teachings to today. But what Jesus wanted and what we have are two very different things. The first great difference was between the quality of Jesus and his disciples. Perhaps St. Peter was the best, but were these Apostles that good? Judas Iscariot was one of the twelve disciples. Peter arrived in Rome in the year 42, where he taught the Word of God. Peter was martyred in year 67 and raised to sainthood. St. Peter was the first Prince of the Apostles—the first Pope. Peter was probably a superior human in social skills and love. But it appears to be downhill from about 350 on. Each Pope was named a Saint for the first 350 years. Then what, I don't know, Rome or civilization changed the goals of spirit or strength of character of the leaders. They got it wrong on the birthday of Christ in 336 A.D. By 1490, the Pope was very human, venal. But the official word was the Pope was without flaw, errorless, and in communication with God. So, were the Popes Pius XI and XII right in their supporting totalitarian rule over people? Were they wrong, or are we, in expecting to live without being controlled totally? If our twentieth-century Popes are capable of errors, flaws then maybe they should alter their declaration of Powers. What should the Protestants do about the differences between peoples ($) and the spirit of goodness between people? Is being a good Christian to others only for those who are saved/Christians? So all the other billions of humans you can treat without scruple? Perhaps make some capitalist gains off of them, as is happening big time this century? Well, God be with you.

For years I thought that Yossarian was like Christ, but it is not so. Yossarian is the master of a new religion. This religion has no God. Christianity, especially as portrayed by chaplain Tappman, is no source of succor, answers, support, or values in these conditions. Finally, our society is portrayed as filled with evil or hopelessly ineffective people. Our social world is weak in values, moral behaviors and strong in Capitalism and the valuation of earning money. My observations of our culture make me agree to 96–7 percent of these portrayals of the book (*Catch-22*). Yossarian meets with a Major psychiatrist. The Major says, "The trouble with you is you think you're too good for all the conventions of society . . . You're a frustrated, unhappy, disillusioned, undisciplined, maladjusted young man!" Yossarian agrees.

Yossarian demonstrates a higher responsibility by running away to Sweden. He thus proves to us that his own (man's) life is sacred.

I realized by the time I was ten years old that our culture was deeply dysfunctional. From the late 1960s on, Tom Robbins wrote of the need for a new religion. Something to replace our current values and morals, he wrote of. Yossarian is my new religious leader.

My opinions follow. Yossarian's friends are his followers/disciples. These are Orr his annoying roommate, Nately the young pilot of Nature, Dunbar his best friend, Hungry Joe the manic sex photographer, Halfoat the Indian humorist, McWatt his pilot, and then later AT Tappman the Group Chaplain. Tappman clearly seems a disciple to his Christ. These are all caring people, some are damaged.

These are compared against men who are normal socially but appear in comparison to be uncaring or evil. I will describe one man, Lt. Milo Minderbinder. Milo is the great world Capitalist, an entrepreneur. Yossarian travels with him once and everywhere they landed Milo was acclaimed with honor all over the region. Milo was given honors of Vice-Shah, Assistant Governor-General, Major Sir Minderbinder, and Gods in uncivilized areas. Yet Milo portrayed greed and selfishness. He had made a bad mistake cornering a market and was losing bundles of money. So, he accepted payment from the NAZI's for bombing his own airbase with U.S. bombers. Milo was killing Americans to maintain his Enterprises.

Yossarian accepts some responsibility for Nately's death and Nately's whore's murderous anger, he sees her as a victim. He wants to save this whore's kid sister from misery and victimization. Every grown victim a culprit and every culprit a victim—

and somebody had to stand up and break the lousy chain. So he tried to. He is deeply moved (down) by the dumb, passive suffering humans he sees in Rome—the blackness of "the shivering, stupefying misery in a world that has never yet provided enough heat, food and justice for all but an ingenious, unscrupulous hand-full."

At the end, the chaplain is with his master. Tappman and a Major, who before was a university professor, advise Yossarian on his choice to make on the Odious Deal. Tappman says, "You must accept it." Yossarian: "I'm not going to do it." He is told that if he does not they will ruin his life. Yossarian tells us that life is all, there is no life after death. He has flown sixty-six combat missions. To fly now would be helping Col. Cathcart and Korn rather than winning the war. "When I look up, I see people cashing in . . . on every decent impulse and every tragedy. I don't see heaven or saints or angels."